KNITTING FROM THE NORTH

Hilary runs her knitwear company from her studio in Orkney. Since 2011 she has been designing winter accessories: hats, mittens and scarves, sending these out to independent boutiques, department stores and customers all over the world, from London to Tokyo.

KNITTING FROM THE NORTH

30 Contemporary Hats, Gloves,
Scarves and Jumpers

Hilary Grant

Photography by Caro Weiss

Kyle Books

First published in Great Britain in 2016 by
Kyle Books, an imprint of Kyle Cathie Ltd
192-198 Vauxhall Bridge Road
London SW1V 1DX
general.enquiries@kylebooks.com
www.kylebooks.com

10 9 8 7 6 5 4 3 2 1

ISBN 978 0 85783 329 7

Designer: Graphical House
Photographer: Caro Weiss
Illustrator: Kuo Kang Chen
Make-up Artist: Sharon Stephens
Project Editor: Sophie Allen
Editorial Assistant: Hannah Coughlin
Production: Nic Jones, Gemma John and Lisa Pinnell

A Cataloguing in Publication record for this title is available from the British Library.

Colour reproduction by ALTA, London
Printed and bound in China by C&C Offset Printing Co., Ltd.

CONTENTS

INTRODUCTION

My studio window looks out onto a large natural harbour, sheltered on all sides by
a group of islands that are huddled amid the wild stretch of ocean where the North
Sea meets the Atlantic. It's a place where cultures meet too – a brackish interweaving
of Nordic and Scottish influences.

This part of the world is the home of Fair Isle knitting, with its inventive, cheerful patterns
and vibrant use of colour. It's not hard to imagine why, in the long dark winters of the
Northern Isles, such an aesthetic tradition might arise. A similar tradition is found across
the Nordic countries too, from Icelandic yokes to iconic Norwegian two-colour knits.

I am not a traditional knitter, but that aesthetic is nevertheless present in my work.
I too find myself gravitating towards bright, cheerful colours and boldly patterned designs
– they seem a necessary response to the winters here. And the rhythm and meter
of Fair Isle knitting remain a constant source of inspiration for me.

For this book, with the help of local hand knitters, I have adapted some of my most
popular machine-knit patterns and designs. Each of the 30 projects use the colour-strand
technique, typical of Fair Isle and Nordic knitting – using two different coloured yarns in
each row. The book covers techniques such as knitting-in-the-round, double-knitting, and
shaping. Also in keeping with this tradition, the styles are simple, practical and timeless.

Some of the projects in this book are small enough to fill an empty afternoon,
others should keep you knitting for weeks. I hope you enjoy these patterns, and that
in reading this book, you will get to know something of the place that inspired them.

TECHNIQUES, KNITWEAR CARE & ABBREVIATIONS

GENERAL NOTES

All patterns require a blunt tapestry needle to sew in yarn ends.

All patterns specify a particular needle size. If your tension differs to that given, adjust your needle size accordingly, particularly when changing from plain stocking stitch to colourwork.

Yarns

All yarn used is *Jamieson's Shetland Spindrift* which is a 4ply 'fingering weight' yarn. It is sold in balls of 25g with a length of approximately 105m per ball. There are websites that can help you find substitutes should you wish to use an alternative, but below are some ideas – please take note that the tension swatch is extremely important if you use a substitute and the weight is referred to as 'fingering weight'.

Rauma, Lamullgarn (93% match)
Malsen Og Mor, Shetland soft (91% match)
Grant Creek Yarns, Cushy Merino 2-Ply (90% match)
Susan Crawford, Fenella 2-ply (90% match)
Sundara Yarn, Fingering Merino (89% match)

Waste Yarn

This is a smooth cotton yarn, ideally in the same weight or ply as the yarn you are using throughout your project. It helps if your waste yarn has a smooth handle and a contrast colour to your main colour as it will be easier to unravel when grafting ends together.

Tension

Tension refers to the number of stitches and rows that make up a 10cm square. It is important to knit a tension swatch before starting your project to ensure it will fit correctly.

Colour Knitting

Colour knitting is when two strands of colour are worked in a single row. When working two strands of yarn it is important to keep an eye on your tension as different patterns can end up worked tighter or looser than is specified in the instructions.

Cast On

Make a slipknot. This is your first stitch. Place on end of left-hand needle and knit into the stitch. Place stitch back onto left-hand needle and repeat the process until you have the number of stitches required as per instructions.

Provisional (invisible) cast-on

You will need one knitting need and one crochet hook. Create a loose slipknot on your crochet hook. With the knitting needle in your left hand, take hold of the tail end of yarn with the left-hand fingers. Holding the crochet hook in your right hand, cross over the knitting needle. Take the working end of the yarn around the back and use the crochet hook to pull the yarn through the loop. This gives you one single cast-on stitch. Repeat the process for as many stitches as required.

Cast Off

Knit 2 stitches. Take 1st stitch on right needle and pass over the 2nd stitch. Knit one stitch and pass the 1st stitch over the 2nd stitch. Repeat this process until you have fully cast off. When the last stitch is on the right needle, take the tail of the yarn and pull through the last stitch to secure. Darn the tail end into the reverse of the knitting and trim the end of the tail.

Knit

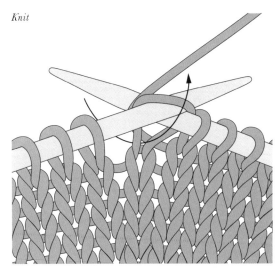

Purl

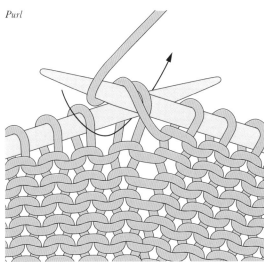

Make One

STITCHES

Knit

With your cast-on stitches on the left-hand needle, place the right-hand needle through the 1st stitch entering the stitch from front to back (needle points away from you). Wrap the yarn around the right-hand needle in an anti-clockwise direction and with the same needle pull the yarn through so that you create a new stitch, which is now on the right-hand needle. Repeat this process.

Purl

Instead of the right-hand needle entering the stitches from front to back, the needle enters from back to front (needle points towards you). Wrap the yarn around the right-hand needle in a clockwise direction, pushing the yarn through the stitch to create a new one, which is now on the right-hand needle.

Make One

Working into the place where the increase is to be made, insert your left needle from the back to the front picking up the bar between the two stitches. Insert the right needle through the 'made' stitch from front to back and knit one stitch. This twists it to create the stitch. If working M1 on purl side, you purl the newly 'made' stitch

Stocking Stitch

Work 1 row in knit and the following 1 row in purl and repeat to create a fabric that has a smooth front. This is usually referred to as the 'right' side of the knitting. When working in rounds, knit every round.

Cast on for Double Knitting

Working Double Knitting

Cast off for Double Knitting

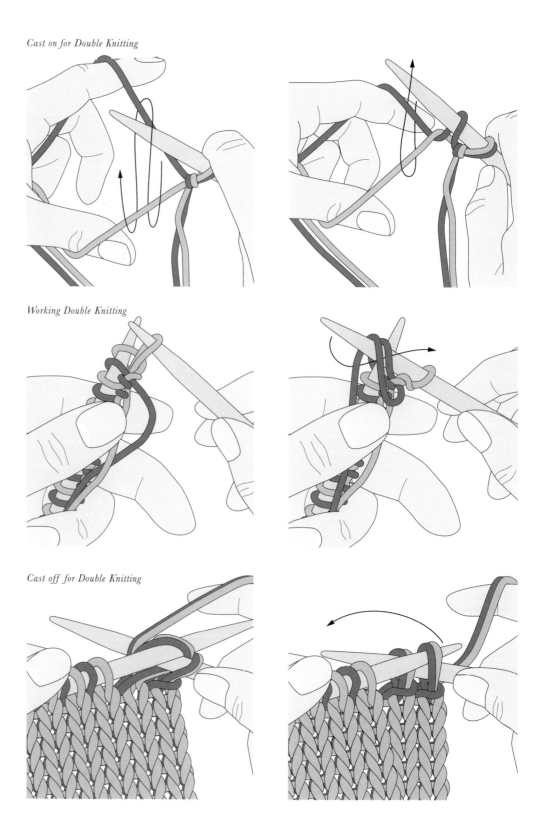

Double Knitting

This technique allows you to create a fabric that has stocking stitch on both sides. Both sides of the row are worked simultaneously, alternating between working Colour 1 as Knit and Colour 2 as Purl. On the next row work Colour 1 as Purl and Colour 2 as Knit. Repeat. As you are working each stitch you must bring both yarns to either the front or the back of the knitting, but you are only working the one yarn in each stitch.

To cast on, take both yarns, make a slipknot and place on left needle. Pay attention to the order of the yarns. You will be casting on each yarn alternatively. Colour 1 is the first colour on the needle. Hold the needle with your right hand. With your left hand you will be holding the yarns, keeping them separate with thumb and forefinger. Colour 1 should be held by forefinger. Colour 2 is held by thumb.

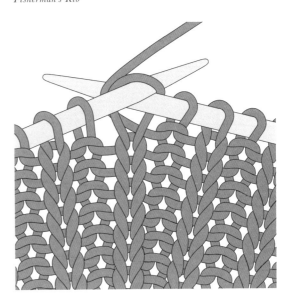

Take the needle towards you over and under Colour 2, away from you and over Colour 1, then towards you under Colour 2 again. That gives you one stitch in Colour 1.

Take the needle behind both yarns, away from you. Take the needle under the Colour 2 and over. Take the needle under Colour 1 and over it. That gives you one stitch in Colour 2.

For an item of width 10 stitches, you would cast on 10 stitches for both colours (20 stitches in total).

To cast off, holding both yarns together, work the first knit-purl stitches together, then work the next knit-purl stitches together. Pass the first stitch over the second as you would on a regular cast off.

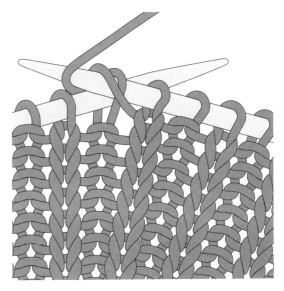

Fisherman's Rib

Fisherman's Rib is always worked over an even number of stitches. It involves working one stitch as a purl and working one stitch below as knit, allowing the stitch above to drop. The process is repeated to the end of the row. When there is a knit stitch at the start or the beginning of the row, the top stitch is worked, instead of working into the stitch below. It creates a very full, stretchy fabric.

Grafting or Kitchener Stitch

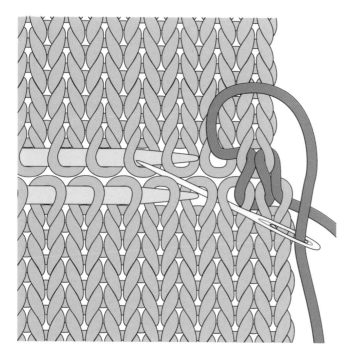

Mattress Stitch

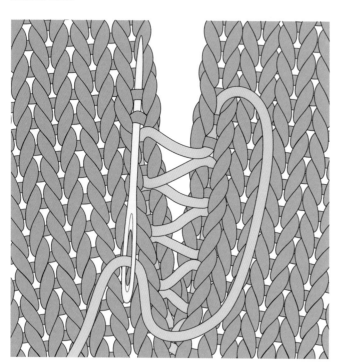

MAKING UP

Grafting or Kitchener Stitch

This is a method to join two pieces of knitting together. It essentially involves sewing a row of knitting in between two raw or live ends.

Lay both ends on a flat surface so that the knit side is facing up and the raw ends/stitches are facing each other. Thread your tapestry needle with MC yarn.

Insert the needles purl-side into the first stitch on the lower piece, then knit-side into the first stitch on the upper piece. Pull the yarn through, ensuring you maintain the same tension as the rest of your knitting.

*Insert the needle knitwise into the first stitch on the lower piece again and pull the yarn through.
Insert the needle purlwise into the next stitch on the lower piece and pull the yarn through.
Insert the needle purlwise into the first stitch on the upper piece and pull the yarn through.
Insert the needle knitwise into the next stitch on the upper piece and pull the yarn through.*

Repeat from * to * until you reach the end of the row.

Mattress Stitch

This is a method of joining two side seams together. It gives you an invisible finish between the two seams. Unlike Kitchener stitch, you work the thread between each stitch, instead of through them. The thread is drawn underneath the 'bar', which is the stitch that runs behind the V-shaped stitch of the right side.

With the knit-side of the piece facing you, lay each side to be joined next to each other, ensuring that the rows are lined up as accurately as possible. You will be working between these end courses of stitches to join them up. Seam the stitches, working from one stitch in from the outside edge, from one side to the other.

Daisy Chain

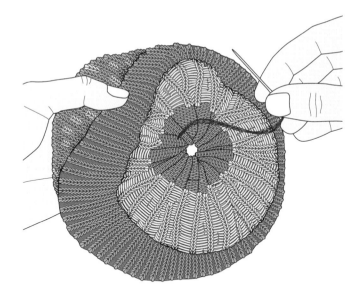

Half-Twist

A half-twist is required to make the twisted effect in the short cowls. If you lay your cowl out on a flat surface, twist one end once so that the side facing you now faces the table. Then join using the technique specified.

FINISHING

Daisy Chain

This is a method similar to running a thread through a stitch but you achieve a more even and secure gather. Take a tapestry needle threaded with a strong thread (topstitch thread plied twice) and sew onto the end of the knitting you wish to gather. Weave the needle in and out of the knitting at 2.5cm intervals and pull in tightly to gather. You will see there is a daisy-like shape made. Then weave the needle in and out of the other ends (which look like tips of petals), pull tightly to gather and secure with a couple of stitches.

Blocking

Blocking is when you manipulate your knitting into shape by wetting the garment, shaping and securing it onto a surface using pins and then setting it in shape either by allowing it to dry naturally or under the heat of an iron.

You can do this straight onto your ironing board, or use specialist blocking mats, if you need a larger surface for blocking a garment. Always check the washing and ironing instructions on your yarn ball band for temperature and care guidance before blocking or pressing your garment.

Blocking a Round Beret

Soak the beret in cold water for 15 minutes. You can add a small amount of softener or non-rinse wool wash if you desire. Insert a round plate, which is slightly larger than the circumference of your hat and position the beret so that the centre of the crown is lined up with the centre of the plate. Ensure that the beret is stretched evenly over the plate and allow to dry in a warm, dry place (but not next to a direct heat source as this may shrink your beret) on top of a towel or sitting on top of a drying horse.

Blocking

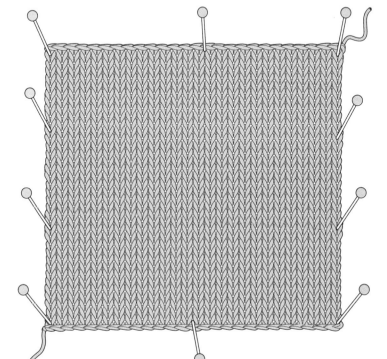

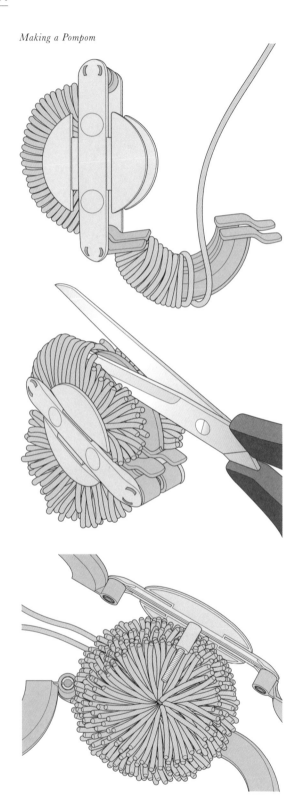

Making a Pompom

You will need:
Pompom maker: 4cm diameter
½ ball of *Jamieson's Shetland Spindrift*

The secret to making a good pompom is having a very dense pile that is trimmed very well. Using your pompom maker of choice, wrap the yarn around each side according to instructions provided. Use topstitch thread plied up 3–4 times to tie your pompom. Holding each end of the topstitch thread, wrap one end around 3 times, creating a triple knot before pulling tightly to ensure the yarns are pulled in well and held securely.

With a pair of sharp scissors, trim your pompom (being careful not to cut off the threads as you will use these to attach it to the hat), turning it constantly to ensure it doesn't end up lop-sided. Have patience with this part and you will have a beautifully round pompom.

To attach your pompom, separate the threads back into their separate ends. Working from the right side of your knitting, sew one group just to the right of the centre of the crown or where your hat has been gathered. Sew on the other group just to the left of the centre of the crown. Open up your hat – you will tie a triple knot which will be concealed within the inside of your hat. Tie another triple knot to be certain. Before trimming the ends, gently tug the pompom to ensure that it is secure and not slack. Trim the ends of the thread inside the hat.

Adding mitten strings

Measure the length of the arms, across the shoulders. This will determine how long your mitten strings need to be. Using a Knitting Dolly, knit a length of cord, using MC yarn. Use instructions specific to the brand/make of your knitting dolly. Ensure you have a generous length rather than too little. If you have too much length you can always knot the cord to shorten it. Secure the ends of the mitten cord to the inside cuff using the MC yarn and a tapestry needle.

KNITWEAR CARE

Taking care of your knitwear is tremendously worthwhile because it will look, feel, smell and fit well for a long, long time. If you have a knitted garment that has stretched out a bit or has lost its lustre, a gentle hand wash and press is usually enough to bring it back to its former glory. I cannot recommend this enough.

I like to have a big hand-wash session about 2–3 times a year where I'll wash everything from cashmere cardigans, wool throws and all my lambswool accessories. I would recommend hand washing particularly for those accessories that come in close contact with your face, such as hats and mittens, which end up getting grubby after a full winter season of make up, pollution and perspiration.

Moths

In most cases you won't see any sign of moths until you open out your favourite jumper when summer is over, only to find holes dotted all over. That is why you need to be really vigilant when it comes to storing and caring for your knitwear.

I don't like to store my knitwear tucked away in my wardrobe, instead I keep it all stored with the rest of my clothing so it can get a bit of fresh air and daily sunlight every morning. If you use wicker baskets to store your knitwear, wash these in the bath every 6 months. For the most precious items, storing in plastic bags in the freezer ensures that no living thing or creature will be able to eat away at your most expensive and loved knitwear.

Cedar wood also acts as a good deterrent. If you have access to a local wood mill, ask if they will sell you some cedar offcuts. Cut them into small pieces, sand off all the rough edges and give it a wipe before placing in your drawer. Or you can drill a hole through one end, tie a length of waxed cord through and hang it up in your wardrobe. Sand the surface occasionally so that you revive the wood and release the smell.

How To Wash Your Knitwear

There are many options available for washing and caring for delicate knitwear and garments. I have tried quite a few and I tend to favour the eco-friendly options as they don't smell too overpowering and are less damaging to the environment. The non-rinse brands are good if you are short of time.

You will need: suitable detergent for wool, rubber gloves, 2–3 large, clean, dry towels and a large, clean basin.

Put on gloves if you have sensitive skin. Fill a clean sink or basin with luke-warm water (it should never feel hot to the skin). Use about a teaspoon of detergent (or as instructed on the detergent label) and swish it around so it disperses in the water.

Place your knitted item in the water, and gently press it down so that it becomes fully submerged and saturated with water. Don't rub your knitwear. Leave it to soak for 5–10 minutes.

Drain all the water away and press as much of the dirty water out of the knitting as you can.

Fill with lukewarm water again and move the knitting around so that you have a chance to rinse away all the suds and dirty water.

Again, drain the basin and press all the water out.

Place on a towel, roll up and gently squeeze to remove all the water. Depending on the size of your garment, you might have to do this more than once, and replace the soaked wet towel with a dry one.

Reshape the knitting on a fresh, dry, flat towel and keep away from direct heat.

Once your knitting has dried, use an iron to gently press into shape. You might have to do a bit of reshaping again. Check the instructions on the ball band or garment label regarding the iron heat level.

ABBREVIATIONS

CC – Contrast Colour

dpns – Double-Pointed Needles

K – Knit

KFB – Knit in front and back

K1b – Knit 1 below

K2 tog – Knit 2 together

MC – Main Colour

M1 – Make 1 stitch by lifting horizontal strand between stitches and knitting into back of it

P – Purl

P2 tog – Purl 2 stitches together

sl1 – Slip 1 stitch without knitting it

sl1-k1-psso – slip stitch, knit next stitch, pass slipped stitch over knitted stitch

sl2-k1-psso – slip 2 stitches together to right-hand needle, knit next stitch, pass 2 slipped stitches over knitted stitch

ssk – Slip, slip knit

st(s) – Stitch(es)

st st – Stocking stitch

BEACON POM HAT

This hat is worked in the round, in K2 P2 rib. This is a slouchy style, but can be worn with a turned-up cuff, for warmer ears and a neater fit. The hat and the pompom look particularly striking, like a bright beacon when created in a single coloured yarn.

Finished Size
Circumference: 45cm, to be worn
with up to 10cm negative ease
Length: 22cm

Yarn
Jamieson's Shetland Spindrift
1 ball *Poppy* (MC)

Needles & Notions
2.75mm circular needle or dpns
Stitch marker

Tension
32 sts x 38 rows = 10 x 10cm
square over unstretched rib

INSTRUCTIONS
Cast on 144 sts and place marker. Join to work in the round.

Work K2, P2 rib for 21cm or desired length.

Next Round: [K2tog, P2] to end of round.
Next Round: [K1, P2tog] to end of round.
Next Round: [K1, P1] to end of round.

Cast off.

FINISHING
Thread tapestry needle with heavy cotton thread.
Daisy chain around top of hat (see page 13), sew in ends
and block.
Make pompom (see page 14) and sew to top of hat.

FISHERMAN'S RIB
FINGERLESS MITTENS

This is a simple project to introduce you to working the Fisherman's Rib stitch. It is dense yet stretchy, which ensures a snug but comfortable fit. Use mattress stitch to seam the mittens together.

Finished Size
Circumference: 18cm when
unstretched – will fit up to
22cm comfortably
Height: 14cm

Yarn
Jamieson's Shetland Spindrift
2 balls *Cobalt*

Needles & Notions
Pair 2.75mm needles

Tension
27 sts x 32 rows = 10 x 10cm

INSTRUCTIONS

Cast on 56 sts, leaving a tail long enough
to use for sewing up.

Work 3 rows in stocking stitch.

Next Row: [K1, P1] across row.
Next Row: [K1b, P1] across row.
Repeat these two rows until work measures 13.5cm
or your desired length.

Work 3 rows in stocking stitch.

Cast off. Break yarn, leaving a tail long enough
to use for sewing up.

FINISHING

Sew side seams together using mattress stitch,
leaving a 3.5cm gap (or longer if required) for
the thumb, 7cm up from the bottom.
Sew in ends and block.

ARROW POM HAT

My Arrow pattern has a bold, simple repeat, making it a good introduction to colour knitting. I have found it is best worked in monochrome, or in strong colours with a white contrast, for a classic Nordic look. This hat is worked in the round and then simply gathered at the crown.

Finished Size
Circumference: 50cm, to be worn
with up to 14cm negative ease
Length: 22cm

Yarn
Jamieson's Shetland Spindrift
        1 ball *Charcoal* (MC)
        1 ball *Natural White* (CC)

Needles & Notions
3mm circular needles
3.25mm circular needles
Stitch marker

Tension
28 sts x 32 rows = 10 x 10cm
square over colourwork using
larger needles

Note
For each round, read chart from
right to left, knit every round.

INSTRUCTIONS
Using MC and smaller needles, cast on 140 sts.
Place marker and join to work in the round,
being careful not to twist.

Work 11 rounds of K1, P1 rib.

Change to larger needles.
Knit 1 round.

Join in CC. Following chart, work 20-st repeat 7 times across
round. Complete chart to end round 51. Break off CC.

Knit 8 rounds.

Cast off.

FINISHING
Daisy chain top of hat (see page 13). Sew in ends.
Make pompom (see page 14) in CC and sew to top of hat.

Chart
MC   *White Square*
CC   *Black Square*

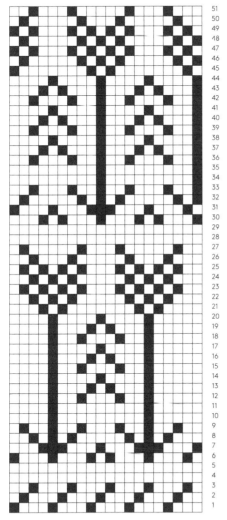

ARROW CUFFS

These little cuffs are worked in the round and are quick to make,
so they will make a good project for an empty afternoon or evening.
These are brilliant for windy days. They stop draughts coming up your
jacket sleeves and they look lovely, layered over the cuffs
of a chunky knit jumper.

Finished Size
Length: 10cm
Circumference: 20cm

Yarn
Jamieson's Shetland Spindrift
       1 ball *Old Gold* (MC)
       1 ball *Natural White* (CC)

Needles & Notions
2.25mm circular needles
2.75mm circular needles
Stitch marker

Tension
30 sts x 36 rows = 10 x 10cm over
colourwork stocking stitch, using
larger needles

Note
For each round, read chart from
right to left, knit every round.

INSTRUCTIONS
Using MC and smaller needles, cast on 60 sts.
Place marker and join to work in the round,
being careful not to twist.

Work 8 rounds of K2, P2 rib.
Change to larger needles.
Next Round: K.

Join in CC.
Following chart, work 10-st repeat 6 times across
round and complete chart to end round 22.

Next Round: Work 1 round in MC.
Change to smaller needles.
Work 8 rounds of K2, P2 rib.

Cast off.

FINISHING
Sew in ends and block.

Chart
MC   *White Square*
CC   *Black Square*

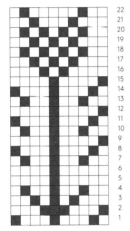

DOT DASH COWL

—

This cowl is worked in the round, with a half-twist and then grafted
so you have a seamless finish. Take your time with the grafting and try
to ensure your stitches are as even as possible. I have used really strong
colours in this pattern – sea blue, green and oxide red,
with crisp white.

Finished Size

Circumference: 64cm
Width: 13cm

Yarn

Jamieson's Shetland Spindrift
   3 balls *Heron* (MC)
   1 ball *Ginger* (CC1)
   1 ball *Natural White* (CC2)
   1 ball *Aqua* (CC3)
   1 ball *Stonewash* (CC4)
   1 ball *Mermaid* (CC5)
Waste yarn

Needles & Notions

3.25mm circular needle
Start of Round Marker (optional)
Dpns in similar size to hold sts
for grafting

Tension

31 sts x 32 rows = 10 x 10cm

Note

For each round, read chart from
right to left, knit every round.

INSTRUCTIONS

Using waste yarn and a provisional method, cast on 80 sts.
Place marker and join to work in the round, being careful
not to twist.

Work through the various charts as follows, repeating
each chart 20 times across the round.

1–12: Using MC and CC1, work Main A. (12 rounds)
13–24: Work Transition A, joining CC2 on third round.
(24 rounds)
25–48: Using MC and CC2, work Main A twice. (12 rounds)
49–60: Work Transition B, joining CC3 on third round.
(12 rounds)
61–84: Using MC and CC3, work Main A twice. (24 rounds)
85–96: Work Transition A, joining CC4 on third round.
(12 rounds)
97–120: Using MC and CC4, work Main A twice. (24 rounds)
121–132: Work Transition B, joining CC5, on third round.
(12 rounds)
133–156: Using MC and CC5, work Main A twice. (24 rounds)
157–168: Work Transition A, joining CC1 on third round.
(12 rounds)
169–180: Using MC and CC1, work Main A once, omitting
final round. (11 rounds)

FINISHING

Unravel the provisional cast on and place the released
sts on dpns. Lay your knitting flat on a table, and fold
so there will be a half-twist (see page 13).
Graft the two ends together using MC.
Darn over the stitches with CC so that the pattern
continues all the way round the scarf.
Sew in ends and block.

Chart
MC   *White Square*
CC1   *Black Square*
CC2   *Grey Square*

MAIN A

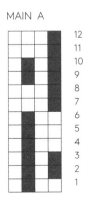

TRANSITION A

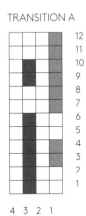

TRANSITION B

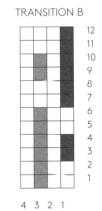

BARLEY FINGERLESS MITTENS

These fingerless mittens are worked in the round. They are quite short
on the fingers, so are well suited for when you need to be both warm
and dexterous. This is another pattern that benefits from
a crisp, bold colourway.

Finished Size
Circumference: 20cm
Length: 16cm

Yarn
Jamieson's Shetland Spindrift
        1 ball *Verdigris* (**MC**)
        1 ball *Natural White* (**CC**)
Waste yarn

Needles & Notions
2.25mm dpns
2.75mm dpns
Stich marker

Tension
40 sts x 40 rows = 10 x 10cm over
colourwork stocking stitch, using
larger needles.

Notes
For each round, read chart from
right to left, knit every round.

In rows where there are blocks of
more than 5 stitches of one colour,
the yarns should be twisted around
each other at the back every few
stitches to prevent any long loops
forming at the back.

INSTRUCTIONS, RIGHT

Using MC and smaller needles, cast on 80 sts. Place marker
and join to work in the round, being careful not to twist.

Work 10 rounds of K2, P2 rib.
Change to larger needles.
Knit 1 round.

Join in CC.
Following chart, work 40-st repeat twice across round,
to end of Round 33.

Round 34: Work chart for 3 stitches. Knit 9 in waste yarn.
Slip these 9 sts back onto left-hand needle, then complete
round following chart pattern.

Complete chart to end Round 43.
Knit 1 round.
Change to smaller needles.
Work 10 rounds of K2, P2 rib.

Cast off.

INSTRUCTIONS, LEFT

Work as for Right to end of Round 33.

Round 34: Work chart for 28 sts. Knit 9 sts in waste yarn.
Slip these 9 sts back onto left-hand needle, then continue
following chart.
Continue working rest of round.

Complete as for Right.

Chart
MC   *White Square*
CC   *Black Square*

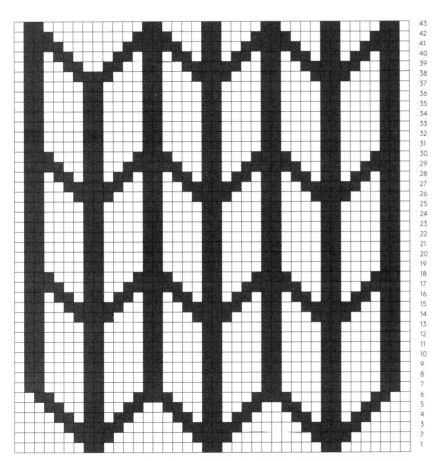

THUMBS

Using smaller needles, pick up the 9 sts both below and above the row of waste yarn – you will have 18 sts over two needles. Very carefully pull the waste yarn out, then transfer sts equally across 4 dpns.
Knit 3cm or to your desired length.

Cast off.

FINISHING

Sew in all ends, closing any small gaps left at base of thumb. Block.

ARROW CIRCLE SCARF

This circle scarf is worked flat and the ends are grafted. It will take a while to work through this pattern but at the end you will have a brilliantly huge, warm scarf that can be worn in a multitude of ways.

Finished Size
Circumference: 150cm
Width: 35cm

Yarn
Jamieson's Shetland Spindrift
        7 balls *Charcoal* (**MC**)
        3 balls *Natural White* (**CC**)
Waste yarn

Needles & Notions
Pair 3mm needles

Tension
30 sts x 32 rows = 10 x 10cm

Note
When working from chart,
odd numbered rows are knit
rows and read from right to left.
Even numbered rows are purl
rows, read from left to right.

INSTRUCTIONS

Using waste yarn and a provisional method, cast on 100 sts.
Using MC, purl 1 row.

Join in CC.
Beginning with a RS row and working in st st throughout,
following chart, work 20-st repeat 5 times across row. Work
the complete chart 8 times, work the chart one final time
to end on Row 51 of chart (475 rows worked in total).
Break off MC leaving approximately 125cm end, to graft
the ends together.

FINISHING

Remove provisional cast on and place sts on a knitting
needle. Graft the 2 ends together using Kitchener
stitch and MC.

Chart
MC   *White Square*
CC   *Black Square*

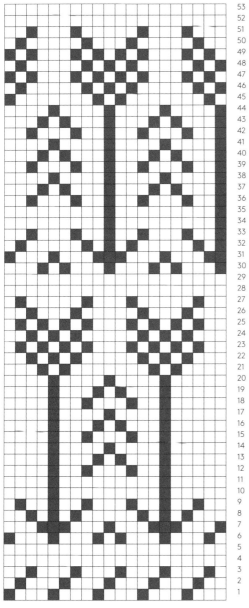

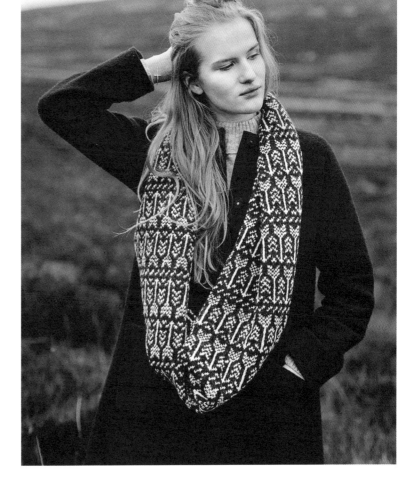

BARLEY TWIST HEADBAND

This is worked on the flat, in double knitting, and has a cable-style twisted plait. The twist is worked by separating the knitting into two cables, which are plaited, and then joined back together. See the Techniques section for more information on double knitting (see pages 10–11).

Finished Size
Circumference: 50cm
Width: 10cm

Yarn
Jamieson's Shetland Spindrift
　　　　1 ball *Heron* (MC)
　　　　1 ball *Natural White* (CC)
Waste yarn

Needles & Notions
Pair 3.75mm needles
3.75mm dpns
2 Stitch holders

Tension
22 sts x 29 rows = 10 x 10cm

Notes
Each square on the chart
represents a pair of stitches, a
knit and a purl. For each square,
knit with the colour shown on the
chart, then purl with the other
colour. Before you knit, you should
bring both yarns to the back of
the work, then before you purl,
you should bring both yarns
to the front of the work.

At the start of each row, the
yarns should be twisted around
each other once to prevent the
work from gaping at the edge.

INSTRUCTIONS
Using waste yarn and a provisional method, cast on 44 sts.
Using the Double Knitting method, work through the chart
for 55 rows.

Add the twist
From the next row you will be working over the first half
of the sts only. Slip the remaining half of the sts to a stitch
holder for ease of working. Continuing to use the Double
Knitting method, work 32 rows of the chart. Slip sts to
a stitch holder. Break off yarns and rejoin at the start of
the remaining sts, and complete as for the first half. Cross
the two halves over once, as per the photo on page 50.

Join the two halves
Transfer all the sts to one needle. You will now work over
all sts. Work 56 more rows following the chart. If you want
to shorten or lengthen the headband here, you should finish
one row short of a full repeat of the chart.

FINISHING
Separate the front and back sides onto two needles.
Remove provisional cast-on and place sts on a knitting
needle, separating the front and back sts. Using the
dominant colour, graft the two 'front' sets of sts together.
Repeat for the 'back' sets. Darn over the sts with the
contrast colour so that the pattern continues all the
way round the scarf. Sew in ends and block.

Chart
MC   *White Square*
CC   *Black Square*

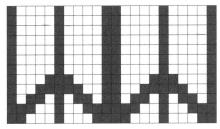

SAXON HAT

This pattern was inspired by a hand-painted stool that was made and handed down through the family. This is knitted in the round and the shaping is done in a single colour, so it's good for beginners. I always top my hats with a pompom, but the crown is shaped and very softly peaked, so it looks just as good without.

Finished Size

Circumference: 52 cm, to be worn with up to 5cm negative ease

Height: 23cm

Yarn

Jamieson's Shetland Spindrift

    1 ball *Heron* (MC)

    1 ball *Granite* (CC1)

    1 ball *Natural White* (CC2)

Needles & Notions

2.75mm circular needles

Stitch markers

Tension

28 sts x 32 rows = 10cm x 10cm over colourwork

Note

For each round, read chart from right to left, knit every round.

INSTRUCTIONS

Using MC, cast on 144 sts. Place marker and join to work in the round, being careful not to twist.

Work 40 rounds of K2, P2, rib.

Knit 3 rounds.

Join CC yarns.

Following chart, work 12-st, repeat 12 times across round.

Complete chart to end Round 28.

Fasten off MC and CC1.

Knit 2 rounds.

Next Round: [Place marker, K9] 16 times.

Next Round: [K to 2 sts before marker, K2tog] to end of round.

Next Round: K.

Repeat these two rounds until 32 sts remain.

Next Round: [K2tog] to end of round.

Next Round: K.

Fasten off, leaving a 20cm end.

FINISHING

Using a tapestry needle, sew end through remaining sts and pull tight. Sew in all ends.

OPTIONAL: Make a pompom (see pages 14) from CC1 and sew to top of hat, ensuring that the pompom conceals the gathered end.

Chart
MC   *Black Square*
CC1   *White Square*
CC2   *Grey Square*

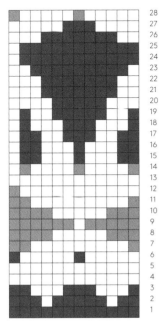

WEFT CUFFS

Like the Arrow Cuffs, these are worked in the round and offer the same warmth and comfort but, as there are three strands worked through, the knit is a little denser and therefore warmer. You can use the colourway I have suggested or make your own using tonal variations of one shade.

Finished Size
Circumference: 20cm
Length: 12cm

Yarn
Jamieson's Shetland Spindrift
      1 ball *Mermaid* (MC)
      1 ball *Stonewash* (CC1)
      1 ball *Caspian* (CC2)
Waste yarn

Needles & Notions
2.25mm circular needles
2.75mm circular needles

Tension
30 sts x 32 rows = 10 x 10cm over colourwork stocking stitch, using larger needles.

Note
For each round, read chart from right to left, knit every round.

INSTRUCTIONS

Using MC and smaller needles, cast on 64 sts. Place marker and join to work in the round, being careful not to twist.

Work 8 rounds of K2, P2 rib.
Change to larger needles.
Next Round: K.

Join in CC yarns.
Following chart, work 8-st repeat 8 times across round.
Complete chart 6 times (24 chart rounds in total).

Next Round: K.
Work 8 rounds of K2, P2 rib.

Cast off.

FINISHING
Sew in ends and block.

Chart
MC   *Grey Square*
CC1   *White Square*
CC2   *Black Square*

ICELANDIC MOCK TURTLENECK

The Icelandic pattern is one of my favourite designs. The turtleneck is worked in the round, before the back and front are separated and worked flat. It has a front and back bib, which, when worn under a coat, gives the impression of being a full jumper. This is a neat and tidy piece to keep your neck and chest warm when you don't want to wear a bulky scarf.

Finished Size
Bib width: 22cm
Bib height: 19cm
Neck rib circumference: 34cm
when unstretched

Yarn
Jamieson's Shetland Spindrift
　　　2 balls *Heron* (MC)
　　　1 ball *Ginger* (CC)

Needles & Notions
2.75mm circular needles
Pair 2.75mm needles
Stitch marker

Tension
27 sts x 35 rows = 10 x 10cm
over colourwork

Note
When working from chart, odd
numbered rows are knit rows, read
from right to left. Even numbered
rows are purl rows, read from
left to right.

INSTRUCTIONS

Using MC and circular needles, cast on 144 sts. Place marker and join to work in the round, being careful not to twist.

Neck
Work 44 rounds of K2, P2 rib.
Next Round: [Cast off 6 sts, K2, P2, K58, P2, K2] twice.

You will now have two sections of 66 sts each.
One will be the Front Bib, the other the Back Bib –
both will be worked the same.

Transfer one of the groups of 66 sts onto a pair of needles.

Bib
Join in CC.
K2, P2, K3, work chart, K2, P2, K2
P2, K2, P3, work chart, P2, K2, P2

Repeat these two rows until chart is complete. Break off CC.
Work one row as set using MC only.

Work 8 rows of K2, P2 rib, starting and ending with K2.
Repeat for second bib.

Cast off. Sew in all ends.

FINISHING
Block after completing second bib.

Chart
MC *White Square*
CC *Black Square*

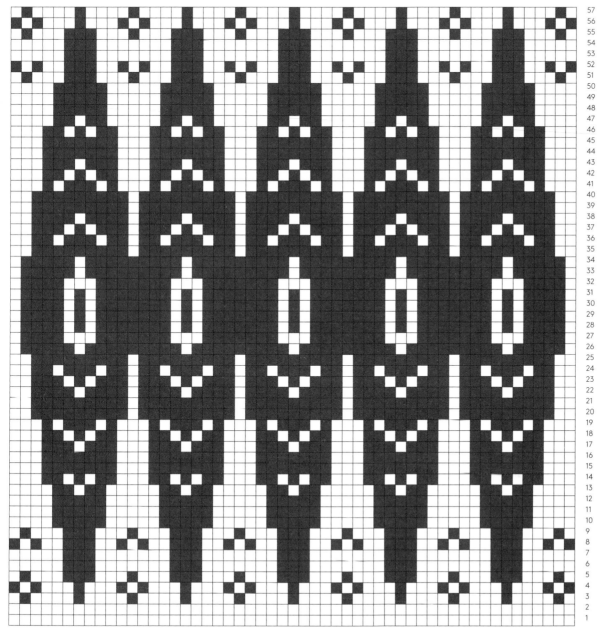

TIDE MITTENS

———

These are in the traditional, pointed Nordic style, which produces a very flat mitten, and an iconic profile. Be aware to weave in your yarns so that the longer strands are worked into the knitting instead of being left loose.

Finished Size
Circumference: 21cm
Length: 22cm

Yarn
Jamieson's Shetland Spindrift
   1 ball *Heron* (MC)
   2 balls *Eggshell* (CC)
Waste yarn

Needles & Notions
2.25mm dpns
2.75mm dpns
Stitch markers

Tension
36 stitches x 40 rows = 10 x 10cm
over colourwork stocking stitch,
using larger needles.

Notes
For each round, read chart from
right to left, knit every round.

Twist CC where there are more
than 5 stitches between MC.

INSTRUCTIONS

RIGHT MITTEN
Using smaller needles and MC, cast on 74 sts.
Work 10 rounds of K1, P1 rib.

Change to larger needles.
Knit 1 round.
Work chart until Round 25.

Round 25: Work 3 sts following chart. Using waste yarn, knit 10 sts. Slip these 10 sts back onto left-hand needle, then continue following chart.

Complete the chart, beginning the top shaping on Round 66 as shown. 22 sts remain.

Break the yarn leaving a 20cm end. Graft sts together using Kitchener stitch.

THUMB
Using smaller needles, pick up the 10 sts both below and above the row of waste yarn – you will have 20 sts over two needles. Very carefully pull the waste yarn out, then transfer sts equally across 4 dpns.

Knit 5cm or to your desired length.

Next Round: [Ssk, K6, K2tog] twice.
Next Round: [Ssk, K4, K2tog] twice.
Next Round: [Ssk, K2, K2tog] twice.
8 sts remain.

Chart
MC   *Black Square*
CC   *Grey Square*
/   *K2tog (knit 2 together)*
\   *SSK (slip slip knit)*

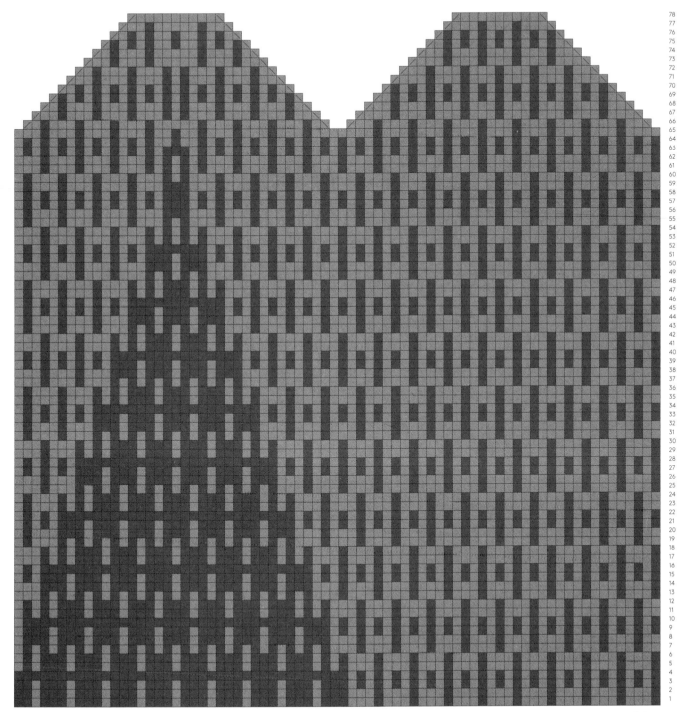

Break the yarn leaving a 20cm end and graft stitches using Kitchener stitch.

LEFT MITTEN
Work as for Right, until Round 25.
Round 25: Work 24 sts following chart. Using waste yarn, knit 10 sts. Slip these 10 sts back onto left-hand needle, then continue following chart.

Complete as for Right.

FINISHING
Sew in ends and block.

BARLEY TWIST SNOOD

This is a nice meditative project to work through. You can work a
gradient through the contrast colour if you like, but I think that the
graphic and clean contrast gives it a fresh and modern Scandinavian feel.
It is knitted in the round, like a tube, twisted and then grafted.

Finished Size
Circumference: 66cm
Width: 16cm

Yarn
Jamieson's Shetland Spindrift
    2 balls *Natural White* (MC)
    2 balls *Bottle Green* (CC)
Waste yarn

Needles & Notions
3.25mm circular needle
Stitch marker (optional)
Dpns in similar size to hold
sts for grafting

Tension
30 sts x 33 rows = 10 x 10cm

Note
For each round, read chart from
right to left, knit every round.

INSTRUCTIONS

Using waste yarn and a provisional method, cast on 96 sts. Place marker and join to work in the round, being careful not to twist.

Join in CC.
Following chart, work 12-st repeat 8 times across round. Work chart 22 times, at the end of the final repeat, omit last round (219 rounds in total). Break off both yarns, leaving a long enough end of MC to graft the ends together.

FINISHING

Unravel the provisional cast-on and place the released sts on dpns. Lay your knitting flat on a table, and fold so there will be a half-twist (see page 13).

Graft the two ends together using MC.

Darn over the stitches with CC so that the pattern continues all the way round the scarf.

Sew in ends and block.

Chart
MC   *White Square*
CC   *Black Square*

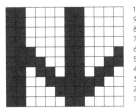

LOKI HAT

This hat is quite a close-fitting style, but it can be made larger
by increasing the number of repeats in the pattern. Knitted in the round
with a shaped crown, this hat features my Loki pattern. It is best
to ensure you have a good level of contrast between your yarns,
either in tone or colour.

Finished Size

Circumference: 46cm to be worn with up to 8cm negative ease
Height: 19cm

Yarn

Jamieson's Shetland Spindrift
1 ball *Cornfield* (MC)
1 ball *Natural White* (CC)

Needles & Notions

2.25mm circular needles
2.75mm circular needles
Stitch marker

Tension

34 sts and 38 rows = 10 x 10cm

Note

For each round, read chart from right to left, knit every round.

INSTRUCTIONS

Using smaller needles and MC, cast on 152 sts. Place marker and join to work in the round, being careful not to twist. Work 10 rounds of K2, P2 rib.

Change to larger needles.
Next Round: [K75, KFB] twice. (154 sts)

Join in CC.
Following chart, work 14-st repeat 11 times across round, beginning decreasing on Round 36. Complete the chart (67 rounds in total).

FINISHING

Cast off and daisy chain remaining 11 sts with heavy cotton thread of a similar colour to your hat (see page 13). Sew in ends.

Chart
MC   *Black Square*
CC   *Grey Square*
/   *K2tog (knit 2 together)*
\   *SSK (slip slip knit)*

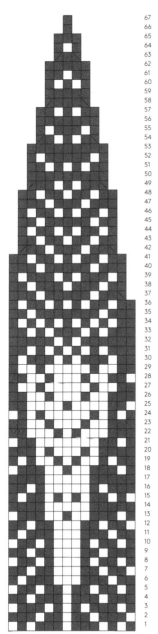

ICELANDIC MITTEN

This mitten has a traditional boxy profile. The ribbed cuff is short,
but you can extend it, if you would like a snugger fit around the wrist.
This pattern is worked in the round, from a rich oxide red and
crisp natural white.

Finished Size
Circumference: 21cm
Length: 20.5cm

Yarn
Jamieson's Shetland Spindrift
      2 balls *Ginger* (MC)
      1 ball *Natural White* (CC)
Waste yarn

Needles & Notions
2.25mm dpns
2.5mm dpns
Stitch marker

Tension
36 sts x 40 rows = 10 x 10cm over colourwork stocking stitch, using larger needles.

Notes
For each round, read chart from right to left, knit every round.

INSTRUCTIONS

RIGHT MITTEN
Using MC and smaller needles, cast on 72 sts. Place marker and join to work in the round, being careful not to twist.

Work K2, P2 for 12 rounds.
Next Round: K.

Join in CC.
Following chart, work 36-st repeat twice until end of Round 23.
Round 24: Work 3 sts following chart. Using waste yarn, knit 10 sts. Slip these 10 sts back onto left-hand needle, then continue following chart.

Complete chart. Break off CC.

Shaping the mitten top
Next Round: Slip marker, K1, ssk, K31, K2tog, place marker, K1, ssk, K31, K2tog.

Next Round: [Slip marker, K1, ssk, K until 2 sts before marker, K2tog] twice. 4 sts decreased.
Repeat last round until 32 sts remain.

Break yarn leaving a 20cm end.
Graft stitches together using Kitchener stitch.

Chart
MC   *White Square*
CC   *Black Square*

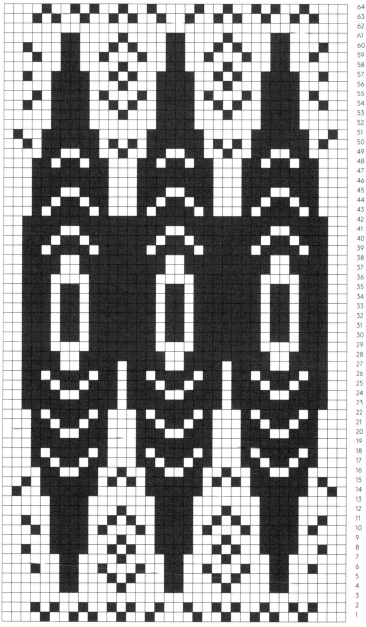

64
63
62
61
60
59
58
57
56
55
54
53
52
51
50
49
48
47
46
45
44
43
42
41
40
39
38
37
36
35
34
33
32
31
30
29
28
27
26
25
24
23
22
21
20
19
18
17
16
15
14
13
12
11
10
9
8
7
6
5
4
3
2
1

36 35 34 33 52 31 30 29 28 27 26 25 24 23 22 21 20 19 18 17 16 15 14 13 12 11 10 9 8 7 6 5 4 3 2 1

Thumb
Using smaller needles, pick up the
10 sts both below and above the row
of waste yarn – you will have 20 sts
over two needles. Very carefully pull
the waste yarn out, then transfer
sts equally across 4 dpns.
Knit 5cm or to your desired length.

Next Round: [K1, ssk, K5, K2tog] twice.
Next Round: [K1, ssk, K3, K2tog] twice.
Next Round: [K1, ssk, K1, K2tog] twice.
8 sts remain.

Break the yarn leaving a 20cm end.
Graft using Kitchener stitch.

LEFT MITTEN
Work as for Right until end of Round 23.
Round 24: Work 22 sts following chart.
Using waste yarn, knit 10 sts. Slip these
10 sts back onto left-hand needle,
then continue following chart.

Complete as for Right Mitten.

FINISHING
Sew in all ends and block.

TIDE BERET

This hat is adapted from my Tide Scarf, which was in my 2014 collection
and uses the same motif as in the Tide Mittens. I've used neutral colours.
You can wear this as a slouchy beanie with the cuff turned down or as a
little beret. This is quite a neat style so if you want to make
it bigger you can increase by one horizontal repeat.

Finished Size
Circumference: 46cm, to be worn
with up to 7cm negative ease
Height: 23cm

Yarn
Jamieson's Shetland Spindrift
  1 ball *Natural White* (MC)
  1 ball *Heron* (CC)

Needles & Notions
2.25mm circular needles
2.75mm circular needles

Tension
32 sts, 42 rows = 10 x 10cm

Notes
For each round, read chart from
right to left, knit every round.

When there is a long run
between MC and CC, twist
yarns every few stitches to ensure
the long floats are secure and the
consistent tension is maintained
in your knitting.

INSTRUCTIONS
Using MC and smaller needles, cast on 144 sts.

Work 9cm of K2, P2 rib.
Change to larger needles.

Next Round: [K3, M1] across round. (192 sts)

Join in CC.
Following chart, repeat 24-st repeat 8 times across round,
working decreases from Round 27.
Complete chart.

FINISHING
Using a tapestry needle, sew end through
remaining sts and pull tight. Sew in all ends.

Block over a form (see page 13).

Chart
MC   *Grey Square*
CC   *Black Square*
/   *K2tog (knit 2 together)*
\   *SSK (slip slip knit)*

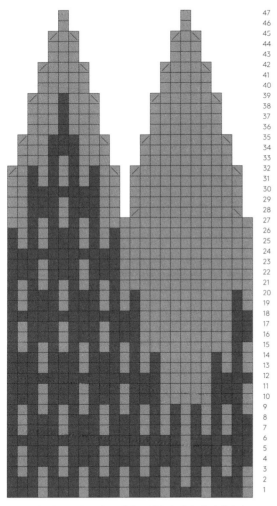

SAXON MITTENS

This is a slightly looser tension to the previous mitts so there are fewer stitches. This will be more of a stretchy style. The fingertips are shaped much like a hat would be when knitted in the round. This should give a softer shape to the end of the mitten. It should also allow the ribbed cuff to have a bit more spring to it and pull in at the wrist for a snug fit.

Finished Size
Fingertip to Wrist: 18cm
Length of cuff (unfolded): 9cm
Circumference: 20cm

Yarn
Jamieson's Shetland Spindrift
  2 balls *Caspian* (MC)
  1 ball *Heron* (CC1)
  1 ball *Granite* (CC2)
Waste yarn

Needles & Notions
2.25mm dpns
2.75mm dpns
Stitch marker

Tension
32 sts x 42 rows = 10 x 10cm over
colourwork stocking stitch, using
larger needles.

Notes
For each round, read chart from
right to left, knit every round.

INSTRUCTIONS

RIGHT MITTEN
Using CC1 and smaller needles, cast on 64 sts. Place marker and join to work in the round, being careful not to twist.

Work 40 rounds K2, P2 rib.
Change to larger needles.
Next Round: [K31, KFB] twice. (66 sts)
Join in MC and work 9 rounds in MC.

Join in CC2. Following chart, work 33-st repeat twice across round, to end Round 17.

Round 18: Work 3 sts following chart. Using waste yarn, knit 10 sts. Slip these 10 sts back onto left-hand needle, then continue following chart.

Complete to end Round 26.
Fasten off CC colours. Work 29 rounds in MC.

Chart
MC   *White Square*
CC1   *Black Square*
CC2   *Grey Square*

SHAPING THE FINGERTIPS

Round 66: [ssk1, K6, ssk1, K13, K2tog, K6 K2tog] twice.
Round 67: K.
Round 68: [ssk1, K5, ssk1, K11, K2tog, K5, K2tog] twice.
Round 69: K.
Round 70: [ssk1, K4, ssk1, K9, K2tog, K4, K2tog] twice.
Round 71: K.
Round 72: [ssk1, K3, ssk1, K7, K2tog, K3, K2tog] twice.
Round 73: K.
Round 74: [ssk1, K2, ssk1, K5, K2tog, K2, K2tog] twice.
Round 75: [ssk1, K9, K2tog] twice.

Break the yarn leaving 20cm end. Graft the stitches together using Kitchener stitch and sew in all ends.

THUMB
Using smaller needles, pick up the 10 sts both below and above the row of waste yarn – you will have 20 sts over two needles. Very carefully pull the waste yarn out, then transfer sts equally across 4 dpns.

Using larger needles, knit 5cm or to your desired length.

Next Round: [ssk, K6, K2tog] twice.
Next Round: [ssk, K4, K2tog] twice.
Next Round: [ssk, K2, K2tog] twice.
8 sts remain.

Break yarn leaving a 20cm end and graft using Kitchener stitch.

LEFT MITTEN
Work as for Right, until end of Round 17.
Round 18: Work 10 sts following chart. Using waste yarn, knit 10 sts. Slip these 10 sts back onto left-hand needle, then continue following chart pattern.

Complete as for Right.

FINISHING
Sew in all ends and block. To add mitten strings see page 14.

BARLEY HAT

This is a variation of my 'Pylon' pattern I designed in 2012. It's been adapted to hand knitting so the strands taken across the back are shorter and therefore easier to work. This hat is worked in the round. The contrast colours are intended to create a gradient effect, using two shades of a single colour.

Finished Size
Circumference: 50cm, to be worn
with up to 10cm negative ease
Height: 23cm

Yarn
Jamieson's Shetland Spindrift
   1 ball *Natural White* (MC)
   1 ball *Verdigris* (CC1)
   1 ball *Bottle* (CC2)
Heavy cotton thread

Needles & Notions
2.75mm circular needles

Tension
28 sts x 32 rows = 10 x 10cm
over colourwork.

Note
For each round, read chart from
right to left, knit every round.

INSTRUCTIONS

Using MC, cast on 140 sts. Place marker and join
to work in the round, being careful not to twist.

Work 10 rounds of K2, P2 rib.
Next Round: K.

Join in CC.
Following chart, work 10-st repeat 14 times across round.
Complete chart to end Round 59.
Fasten off colours.

Cast off in MC.

FINISHING

Using a tapestry needle and heavy cotton thread
in a similar colour to MC, daisy chain around top of hat (see
page 13).
Sew in ends and block.

Make a pompom (see page 14) in CC2 and sew onto top
of hat, ensuring that the pompom conceals the gathered
end and is secured tightly.

Chart
MC   *White Square*
CC1   *Grey Square*
CC2   *Black Square*

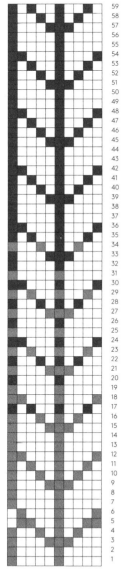

DOT DASH HEADBAND

This headband involves Double Knitting, which is quite a challenging technique, but it is well worth persevering with (see pages 10–11). It involves working a knit stitch on both sides, making for a thick, stretchy and fully reversible fabric – perfect for a headband.

Finished Size
Headband: 52cm
Width: 12cm

Yarn
Jamieson's Shetland Spindrift
          1 ball *Aqua* (MC)
          1 ball *Heron* (CC)
Waste yarn

Needles & Notions
Pair 3.75mm needles
Pair 3mm needles

Tension
Headband Tension: 23 sts,
27 rows to 10cm
Knot Tube Tension: 26 sts
and 36 rows = 10 x 10cm

Notes
Each square on the chart
represents a pair of stitches,
a knit and a purl. For each square,
knit with the colour shown on the
chart, then purl with the other
colour. Before you knit, you should
bring both yarns to the back of
the work, then before you purl,
you should bring both yarns
to the front of the work.

At the start of each row, the
yarns should be twisted around
each other once to prevent the
work from gaping at the edge.

INSTRUCTIONS

HEADBAND
When looking at the chart, each square represents both
a knit and a purl stitch. Twist the yarns around each other
at the start of every row to ensure that the edges fit
together without gaping.

With both MC and CC held together, and using larger
needles, cast on 27 sts.

Following chart, work 6-st repeat 9 times across row.
Complete chart 9 times (144 rows worked in total). If you
want a larger or smaller headband, work more or fewer
repeats of the chart – remembering you will need more
yarn if making it larger.

To cast off, holding both yarns together, knit the first knit-
purl pair of sts together, and then knit the next knit-purl
pair together. Then pass the first st over the second as
you would for a regular cast off.

KNOT TUBE
The knot will be knitted in single knit. It's important that
the knot isn't as bulky, as we want it to pull in the headband
piece and not create too much thickness at the top of
the head.

Using waste yarn, smaller needles and a provisional method,
cast on 20 sts. Using MC, work 11cm in stocking stitch.

Remove provisional cast-on and place sts on a knitting
needle. Graft the two ends together using Kitchener
stitch and MC.

Chart
MC   *White Square*
CC   *Black Square*

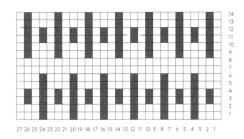

FINISHING

Block both pieces. The sides of the Knot Tube should curl in slightly. Thread the Headband through the Knot Tube. Seam the two ends of the headband together.

Referring to the diagram, use a tapestry needle and MC to sew point A to B and point C to D together securely.

This will create an even-gathered effect at the centre of your headband.

Pull the Knot Tube around so that it is centred over the seam covering the stitches.

grafted seam

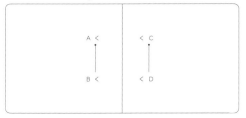

FISHERMAN'S RIB
MOCK TURTLENECK

The fabric is created using Fisherman's Rib technique, which is dense yet stretchy, and so ideal for this style, fitting snugly around the neck and shoulders. It has been designed as an alternative to scarves for when you just need an extra bit of warmth without the bulk.

Finished Size
Bib width: 22cm
Bib length: 17cm
Neck rib circumference: 34cm
when unstretched

Yarn
Jamieson's Shetland Spindrift
3 balls *Natural White*

Needles & Notions
2.75mm circular needles
Pair 2.75mm needles

Tension
27 sts x 32 rows = 10 x 10cm over
Fisherman's Rib

Notes
Read chart from right to left on
RS rows, left to right on WS rows.

INSTRUCTIONS
Using circular needles cast on 144 sts.

Work 43 rounds of P2, K2 rib (start with P2 to match pattern
further on in the work).

Next Round: [Cast off 6 sts, K2, P2, K58, P2, K2] twice.

You will now have two sections of 66 sts each. One will
be the Front Bib, the other the Back Bib – both will be worked
the same.

Transfer one of the groups of 66 sts onto a pair of needles.

Bib
Next Row: K2, P2, K1, [P1b, K1] until 4 sts remain, P2, K2.
Next Row: P2, K2, P1, * [K1, P1] * rep * to * until end of row.

Repeat these two rows 33 times.
Work 3 rows of K2, P2 rib, starting and ending with K2.

Cast off.

Repeat for second section of sts.

FINISHING
Sew in ends and block.

WAVE FINGERLESS MITTENS

These mittens are long on both the fingers and the wrists, so they are particularly warm. They are worked in the round, with the thumbs worked in on waste yarn.

Finished Size
Circumference: 20cm
Length: 26cm

Yarn
Jamieson's Shetland Spindrift
      2 balls *Aqua* (**MC**)
      1 ball *Natural White* (**CC**)
Waste yarn

Needles & Notions
2.75mm dpns
3mm dpns

Tension
29 sts x 38 rows = 10 x 10cm over
colourwork stocking stitch, using
larger needles.

Note
For each round, read chart from
right to left, knit every round.

INSTRUCTIONS

RIGHT MITTEN

Using MC and smaller needles, cast on 56 sts. Place marker and join to work in the round, being careful not to twist.

Work 30 rounds of K2, P2 rib.
Change to larger needles.

Next Round: [K27, KFB] twice. (58 sts)
Next Round: K.

You will have a plain vertical column of stitches separating the start and the end of the chart in every circular row.
*K1 in MC before starting chart.
Join in CC.
Following chart, work 27-st repeat.*
Repeat * to * until end of Round 37.

Round 38: Work 3 sts following chart. Using waste yarn, knit 8 sts. Slip these 8 sts back onto left-hand needle, then continue following chart.

Complete chart to end Round 56. Break off CC.

Next Round: [K27, K2tog] twice. (56 sts)
Next Round: K.

Change to smaller needles.
Work 10 rounds in K2, P2 rib.

Cast off.

Chart
MC   *White Square*
CC   *Black Square*

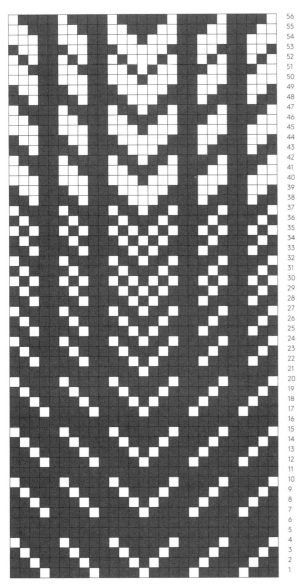

LEFT MITTEN

Work as for Right to the end of Round 37.

Round 38: Work 18 sts following chart. Using waste yarn, knit 8 sts. Slip these 8 sts back onto left hand needle, then continue following chart.

Complete as for Right.

THUMBS

Using smaller needles, pick up the 8 sts both below and above the row of waste yarn – you will have 16 sts over two needles. Very carefully pull the waste yarn out, then transfer stitches equally across 4 dpns.

Work 3cm or to your desired length.

Cast off.

FINISHING

Sew in all ends, closing any small gaps left at base of thumb. Block.

ICELANDIC HAT

This design is inspired by the structured motifs of Icelandic jumper yokes.
I created it back in 2012 when I had just moved to Orkney and was really inspired
by the knitting from Scandinavian and Nordic countries. The hat is worked in the round
and is shaped towards the crown. I think it looks best in really classic Nordic colours –
oxide red, indigo or black – with a white contrast.

Finished Size
Circumference: 56cm, to be worn
with up to 5cm negative ease
Height: 22cm including unfolded
ribbed brim

Yarn
Jamieson's Shetland Spindrift
          1 ball *Prussian* (MC)
          1 ball *Natural White* (CC)
Waste yarn

Needles & Notions
2.75mm circular needles

Tension
30 sts and 32 rows = 10 x 10cm
over colourwork

Note
For each round, read chart from
right to left, knit every round.

INSTRUCTIONS
Using MC, cast on 160 sts. Place marker and join to work
in the round, being careful not to twist.

Work K2, P2 rib for 9cm.
Knit 2 rounds.

Join in CC.
Following chart, work 10-st repeat 16 times across round.
Complete chart, working decreases from Round 21, to end
Round 43.

Using CC knit 1 round.
Next Round: K2tog 16 times.
Cast off remaining sts.

FINISHING
Using a tapestry needle and heavy cotton thread in a similar
colour to MC, daisy chain top of hat (see page 13).

Make a pompom (see page 14) and sew onto top of hat,
ensuring that the pompom conceals the gathered end
and is secured tightly. Sew in ends and block.

Chart
MC   *White Square*
CC   *Grey Square*
/   *K2tog (knit 2 together)*
\   *SSK (slip slip knit)*

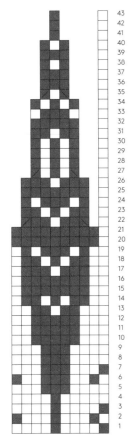

LOKI CIRCLE SCARF

This is a slightly shorter version of the other circle scarves. This project has quite a large vertical repeat, and is one of the more complicated patterns in this book, but the resulting effect is striking even from a distance. The circle scarf is worked flat so there is enough drape to sit well on the shoulders. I've used a saturated yellow with a crisp natural white yarn for maximum impact, but the colours can always be substituted if you are little less bold with colour.

Finished Size
Circumference: 120cm
Width: 19cm

Yarn
Jamieson's Shetland Spindrift
       2 balls *Cornfield* (**MC**)
       2 balls *Natural White* (**CC**)
Waste yarn

Needles & Notions
Pair 3mm needles

Tension
29 sts x 30 rows = 10 x 10cm

Note
When working from the chart, odd numbered rows are knit rows and read from right to left. Even numbered rows are purl rows and read from left to right.

INSTRUCTIONS

Using provisional method and waste yarn, cast on 55 sts. Join in MC and CC.
Following chart, work 55-st pattern once, repeating chart 5 times, omitting the last row on the final repeat (359 rows in total).

FINISHING

Unravel the provisional cast-on and place the released sts on a knitting needle.

Graft the two ends together using MC.

Darn over the stitches with CC so that the pattern continues all the way round the scarf.

Sew in ends and block.

Chart
MC   *White Square*
CC   *Black Square*

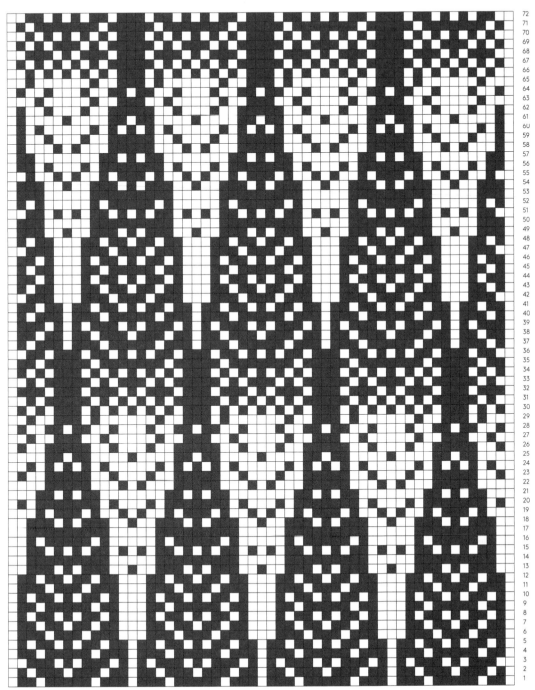

72
71
70
69
68
67
66
65
64
63
62
61
6U
59
58
57
56
55
54
53
52
51
50
49
48
47
46
45
44
43
42
41
40
39
38
37
36
35
34
33
32
31
30
29
28
27
26
25
24
23
22
21
20
19
18
17
16
15
14
13
12
11
10
9
8
7
6
5
4
3
2
1

55 54 53 52 51 50 49 48 47 46 45 44 43 42 41 40 39 38 37 36 35 34 33 32 31 30 29 28 27 26 25 24 23 22 21 20 19 18 17 16 15 14 13 12 11 10 9 8 7 6 5 4 3 2 1

TRIANGLES GLOVES/MITTENS

This project has a number of different options in the finished style.
Due to the placement of the motif, the glove is worked flat and
then joined at the sides.

Finished Size
Palm circumference: 21cm

Yarn
Jamieson's Shetland Spindrift
      2 balls *Granite* (MC)
      1 ball *Sea bright* (CC1)
      1 ball *Ginger* (CC2)

Needles & Notions
Pair 2.25mm needles
Pair 2.75mm needles
2.25mm dpns
Stitch holders
Stitch markers

Tension
36 sts x 42 rows = 10 x 10cm
over colourwork stocking stitch,
using larger needles.

Notes
When working from the chart,
odd numbered rows are knit rows
and read from right to left. Even
numbered rows are purl rows and
read from left to right.

You will find it easier if you use
bobbins with small amounts of
yarn wound onto them for areas
of colour.

INSTRUCTIONS

SHORT-FINGERED GLOVES, RIGHT
Using CC1 and smaller needles, cast on 74 sts.

Row 1 (RS): K, work K2, P2 to last stitch, K1.
Row 2 (WS): P1, work K2, P2 to last stitch, P1.
Repeat these two rows until work measures 8cm,
ending on a WS row.

Change to larger needles.
Join in MC.

Next Row: K1 MC, work across chart twice, K1 MC.
Next Row: P1 MC, work across chart twice, P1 MC.
Work as set until end of Row 24.

Row 25: K1 MC, K38 sts in pattern, knit the next 10 sts on
a piece of waste yarn. Slip the last 10 sts just knitted back
onto the left-hand needle and knit in pattern as on the
chart to last st, K1 MC.
Fasten off CC yarns.
Work stocking stitch until work measures 11cm
from end of rib, ending with a WS row.

Fingers
Little finger: Using MC, K2tog, K8, slip next 54 sts onto
a stitch holder, cast on 2 sts, K8, K2tog. Slip these 20 sts
to smaller dpns. Join to work in the round and knit 8 rounds.
Cast off loosely. Break yarn.

Chart
MC   *White Square*
CC1   *Black Square*
CC2   *Grey Sqaure*

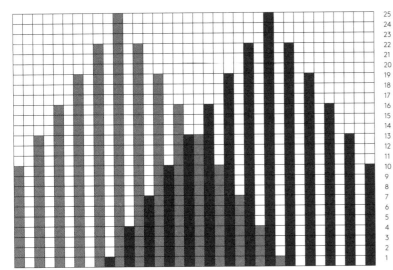

36 35 34 33 32 31 30 29 28 27 26 25 24 23 22 21 20 19 18 17 16 15 14 13 12 11 10 9 8 7 6 5 4 3 2 1

Ring finger: Slip the next 9 sts from front of glove, and 9 sts from back onto smaller needles. Pick up 2 sts from the cast-on edge of the little finger over the gap – 20 sts in total. Knit 10 rounds. Cast off loosely. Break yarn.

Middle and index fingers: Work as for the ring finger, picking up 2 sts from the cast-on edge of previous finger.

Thumb
Using smaller needles, pick up the 10 sts both below and above the row of waste yarn – you will have 20 sts over two needles. Very carefully pull the waste yarn out, then transfer stitches equally across 4 dpns. Pick up 1 st at each end of the hole – 22 sts in total. Knit 8 rounds. Cast off loosely.

LEFT
Work as for Right, apart from Row 25: Row 25: K1 MC, K 24 sts in pattern, knit the next 10 sts using waste yarn. Slip the last 10 sts just knitted back onto the left-hand needle, work chart to last st, K1 MC.

FINISHING

Sew in ends and, if necessary, use MC to darn any small gaps that may have been left at the base of fingers. Using appropriately coloured yarn, use mattress stitch to sew an invisible seam exactly one stitch in from the edge, sewing from the base of the little finger to the bottom of the rib.

FULL FINGERED GLOVES

Use the same pattern for short-fingered gloves, but work the fingers to the following lengths (or adjust to your finger lengths as necessary):
Little finger: 5.5cm
Ring finger: 7cm
Middle finger: 7.5cm
Index finger: 7cm
Thumb: 5cm

Do not cast off but close as follows:
Fingers:
Round 1: [K2tog, K2] 5 times.
Round 2: K.
Round 3: K2tog to last st, K1.
Break off yarn, draw through sts and fasten off.

Thumb:
Round 1: [K2tog, K2] 5 times, K2tog.
Round 2: K
Round 3: K2tog to end.
Break off yarn, draw through sts and fasten off.

MAKING CONVERTIBLE GLOVES WITH REMOVABLE MITTEN TOP

This style is adaptable for when a little more dexterity is needed. The top of the mitten and the thumb can be slid on and off as required.

Work Short-Fingered Glove pattern, then add the Glove top and Thumb top to each glove.

Glove Top

With smaller dpns, starting at seam edge, and four rows below start of fingers, pick up a loop from each stitch across back of hand for 36 sts, place marker, cast on 36 sts, place marker. Join to work in the round.

Rounds 1–4: Knit to marker, slip marker, work, K2 P2 rib to marker, slip marker. Work stocking stitch across all sts until work measures 4.5cm from start of glove top.

Shape top:

Round 1: [K1, ssk, K to 2 sts before marker, K2tog, K1] twice.
Round 2 and all even rounds: K.

Repeat these two rounds until 36 sts remain. Graft sts together using Kitchener stitch.

Thumb Top

With smaller dpns, pick up 12 sts on the outer side of the thumb, four rows below cast-off. Cast on 12 sts and join to work in the round.

Rounds 1–4: K12, K12 in K2, P2 rib.

Rounds 5–16: K.

Shape top:

Round 1: [K2tog, K2] 6 times.
Round 2: K.
Round 3: [K2tog] 6 times.

Break off yarn, draw through sts and fasten off.

WAVE CIRCLE SCARF

Wave was inspired by the patterns in the water in Houton Bay, Orkney. On the rare occasion when the sea is calm flat, the wake from the ferries nearby comes into the bay in a really uniform rhythm with shallow peaks almost strobing along the surface of the water. This is knitting on the flat again, required to provide a fluid drape around the shoulder and grafted to create a continuous loop. The project has quite a large pattern repeat, which is uncommon in hand knitting, but which gives you a really striking result.

Finished Size
Circumference: 135cm
Width: 20cm

Yarn
Jamieson's Shetland Spindrift
       3 balls *Verdigris* (MC)
       2 balls *Natural White* (CC)
Waste yarn

Needles & Notions
Pair 3mm needles

Tension
28 sts x 29 rows = 10 x 10cm

Note
When working from the chart,
odd numbered rows are knit rows
and read from right to left. Even
numbered rows are purl rows and
read from left to right.

INSTRUCTIONS

Using provisional method and waste yarn, cast on 55 sts. Work through the chart 7 times, omitting the last row of the final repeat to end Row 391.

FINISHING

Unravel the provisional cast-on and place the released sts on a knitting needle. Graft the two ends together using MC. Darn over the sts with CC so that the pattern continues all the way round the scarf. Sew in ends and block.

Chart
MC   *Black Square*
CC   *White Square*

ICELANDIC JUMPER

This jumper is worked from the neck down, and in the round for the
yolk, the body and the sleeves. It is very important to check your tension
and measurement throughout. The ribbed cuffs on the sleeves are long
enough to be turned up, to create a really snug and windproof
fit around the wrists.

To Fit	Small (8–10)	Medium (12–14)	Large (16–18)
Body circumference (in cm)	92	99	106
Body length (top shoulder to hem) in cm	55	56	57
Neck (in cm)	35	37	39
Sleeves at bicep (in cm)	31	34	38
Sleeves at wrist (in cm)	20	21	22

Yarn

Jamieson's Shetland Spindrift

11(11, 13) balls *Heron (MC)*
3 (3,4) balls *Poppy (CC)*

Waste yarn

Needles & Notions

3mm circular needles
2.5mm circular needles
Stitch holders
Stitch markers

Tension

36 sts x 42 rows = 10 x 10cm over colourwork stocking stitch, using larger needles.

Notes

For each round, read chart from right to left, knit every round.
When choosing size, jumper should be worn with approx. 10cm positive ease.
Where only one number is given, it applies to all sizes.

INSTRUCTIONS

Yoke

Using MC and larger needles, cast on 100 (108, 116) sts loosely. Place marker and join to work in the round.
Work K2, P2 rib for 2cm. K one round.

Next Round: [K2, M1] across round. (150 (162, 174) sts)
Knit until work measures 5cm from start of ribbing.

Next Round: [K2, M1] across round. (225 (243, 261) sts)
Knit until work measures 10cm from start of ribbing.

Next Round: [K3, M1] across round. (300 (324, 348) sts)
Knit until work measures 15 (15, 16)cm from start of ribbing.

Next Round: K3 (0, 5), *M1, K4 (4, 3), M1, K5 (4, 4); repeat from * across round. (366 (405, 446) sts)
Knit until work measures 20 (21, 22)cm from start of ribbing.

Size M only: K to end of round, M1. 406 sts.
Size L only: [K221, K2tog] twice.

Remove start of round marker.

Chart
MC   *White Square*
CC   *Black Square*

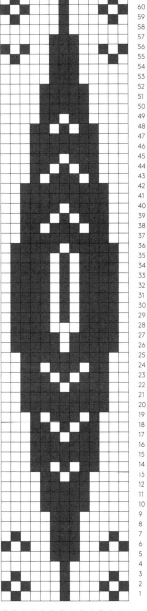

Divide Body and Sleeves

*K113 (123, 133) sts, slip next 70 (80, 90) sts to stitch holder for sleeve, cast on 10 sts, place marker, cast on 10 sts; repeat from * across round. (266 (286, 306) sts)

You will now be working the Body, the Front and Back sts being separated by markers.

Join in CC.

*Slip marker, work the first st of the chart, work the marked 13-st repeat 13 (14, 15) times, then work the final 2 sts of chart. Repeat from * once more.

Work through the 61 rounds of the chart as set then break off CC. Knit until work measures 35cm from underarm, or 4cm short of desired length.

Next Round: [K131 (141, 151), K2tog] twice. (264 (284, 304) sts)

Using smaller needles, work 4cm of K2, P2 rib.

Cast off loosely.

WORKING THE SLEEVES

Transfer the held sleeve sts onto larger needles. Pick up and knit 20 sts from the cast-on edge at the underarm, placing marker at centre of these sts to mark start of round. (90 (100, 110) sts)

Knit 1 round.

Working marked repeat only, work through chart, repeating 9 (10, 11) times across the round.

Shape the sleeve

Decrease Round: ssk, K until 2 sts rem, K2tog.

Work Decrease Round every 6th round, 10 (7, 18) times. (70 (86, 74) sts)

Work Decrease Round every 4th round, 7 (13, 5) times. (56 (60, 64) sts)

Knit until work measures 41 (42, 43) cm from underarm – or desired length until start of ribbing.

Using smaller needles, work 13cm (or desired length) of K2, P2 rib.

Cast off loosely.
Repeat for other sleeve.

FINISHING

Sew in ends and, if necessary, use MC to darn any small gaps that may have been left at the underarm joins.

In wear, fold sleeve cuffs up.

LOKI JUMPER

———

This jumper is worked in the round from the waist up.
It has a dropped shoulder to give a loose fit on the body, but the ribbed
arms are intended to have a snug fit. It is very important to measure
your knitting throughout, to ensure a consistent garment width,
in the sections both of colour and of plain knitting.

To Fit	Small (8–10)	Medium (12–14)	Large (16–18)
Body circumference (in cm)	100	110	120
Body length (top shoulder to hem) in cm	57	58	59

To be worn with up to 20cm positive ease

Yarn

Jamieson's Shetland Spindrift
11 (11, 13) balls *Dove* (MC)
3 (3, 4) balls *Natural White* (CC)

Needles & Notions

2.5mm circular needles
3mm circular needles
2.5mm circular needles or dpns
Stitch holders
Stitch markers

Tension

26 sts x 30 rows = 10 x 10cm
over stocking stitch, using larger
needles.

Note

For each round, read chart from
right to left, knit every round.

INSTRUCTIONS

Body

Using MC and smaller needles, cast on 256 (284, 312) sts.
Place marker and join to work in the round. Work K2,
P2 rib for 4cm.

Change to larger needles.

Next Round: Slip marker, M1, work 128 (142, 156) sts for the
Front, place marker, M1, work 128 (142, 156) sts for the Back.
(258 (286, 314) sts)

Next Round: *Slip marker, K1 MC, work first 0 (7, 0) sts
of chart, work marked repeat 9 (9, 11) times, work the final
1 (8, 1) sts of chart, K1, MC. Repeat from * once more.

Work through the 100 rounds of the chart as set then break
off CC. Knit in MC only until work measures 37cm from
cast-on edge, or to desired length up to underarm.

Front

Next Round: SM, K to next M, remove marker. Place
remaining sts on holder for the Back. (129 (143, 157) sts)

Starting with a purl row, work in stocking stitch for 12
(13, 14)cm, ending after a purl row.

Next Row: K49 (53, 58) sts, and put these on holder for
Left shoulder, K31 (37, 41) sts, and put these on holder
for the Front Neck, K to end of row.

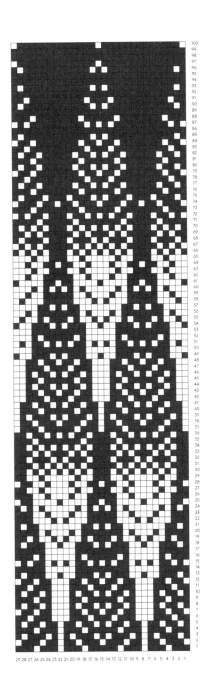

Right Shoulder
Next Row: P.
Next Row: K1, ssk, knit to end of row.

Repeat the last two rows 8 times more.
40 (44, 49) sts rem. Work in stocking stitch until work measures 20 (21, 22)cm from start of armhole. Leave sts on holder.

Left Shoulder
With WS facing, return to sts held for Left Shoulder. P 1 row.

Next Row: K to last 3 sts, K2tog, K1.
Next Row: P.

Repeat the last two rows 8 times more.
40 (44, 49) sts remain. Work in stocking stitch until work measures 20 (21, 22)cm from start of armhole. Leave sts on holder.

Back
Return to sts held for the Back.
Work in stocking stitch until work measures same as Front from the start of armhole.
Next Row: K40 (44, 49) sts, and place on holder for the Right Shoulder, K49 (55, 59) sts and put on holder for the Back Neck, K to end of row. With WS facing, work a 3 needle cast-off across the shoulders. Turn right sides out.

Neck
Using MC and circular needle or dpns, pick up and knit 10 sts down the left side of front neck, knit across the held 31 (37, 41) sts for the front of neck, pick up and knit 10 sts up the right side of neck, knit across the held 49 (55, 59) sts at back of neck. (100 (112, 120)sts)

Work in K2, P2 rib for 3cm. Cast off loosely in pattern.

SLEEVES
Using MC and smaller circulars or dpns, and starting at the underarm, pick up and knit 52 (54, 56) sts from each of the Front and Back armhole. Place marker to show start of round. (104 (108, 112) sts)

Work 1 round in K2, P2 Rib.
Next Round: Work 2tog, work in patt until 2 sts remain, work 2tog.
Next Round: Work in patt as set.
Repeat these two rounds until 68 (76, 84) sts remain.
Work 8cm in rib.
Next Round: Work 2tog, work in patt until 2 sts remain, work 2tog.
Work 3 rounds in patt as set.
Repeat these four rounds until 40 (40, 44) sts remain.

Work in rib until sleeve measures 37 (39, 41)cm, or desired length, from underarm.
Cast off loosely.

FINISHING
Sew in all ends, and block.

INDEX

ACKNOWLEDGEMENTS

Firstly, I would like to thank Judith Hannam and Sophie Allen for giving me the opportunity to write a knitting book and for all their guidance throughout the entire process.

Caro Weiss our amazing photographer, there are no limits to her talent, and enthusiasm no matter how muddy, cold or windy the location. http://www.caroweiss.com

Louise Barrington and Vendella Gebbie, our lovely models who brought the knitwear to life and fun and laughs throughout the long, chilly days shooting on location.

Sharon Stephens our make up artist on the shoot who is so skilled in bringing out the best in people. Thank you to Sharon for looking after us all with her Mary Poppins bag of endless supplies. http://www.sharonstephen.com

Sarah Moar a retired English teacher and obsessive hand knitter who knitted many of the pieces in this book. Knitting pattern instructions would often come back from Sarah peppered with grammatical and spelling corrections – with alternate suggestions in the margins.
Thank you Sarah!

Thank you to our other amazing knitter, Ivy Kemp. Ivy will knit anything, no matter how big, complicated or difficult. She's been known to visit the local welders to have her knitting needles extended for her more ambitious projects!

Thank you Jamieson's of Shetland who provided the beautiful 100% Shetland yarn.

Kerrie Aldo, whose beautiful hand made waxed cotton coats were worn in the photoshoots. These coats were perfect for keeping out the cold winds on the Orkney cliff tops and complemented the knitted garments perfectly. www.kerrialdo.com

RESOURCES

Yarn Brands
Jamieson's of Shetland www.jamiesonsofshetland.co.uk
Woolfolk Yarn www.woolfolkyarn.com
New Lanark Wool www.newlanarkshop.co.uk
UK Alpaca www.ukalpaca.com
Guernsey Wool www.guernseywool.co.uk

Knitting Shops EU & UK
Fluph www.fluph.co.uk
Love Knitting www.Loveknitting.com
The Quernstone, Stromness, Orkney. If you are ever in Orkney this shop has an absolutely brilliant selection of yarns, needles and notions.
Ba Ram Ewe – Yorkshire www.baaramewe.co.uk
Loop www.loopknittingshop.com

Knitting Shops US
Purl Soho www.purlsoho.com
Fringe Supply Co (excellent selection of knitting bags, zines and sheep related goods.) www.fringesupplyco.com
Tolt Yarn and Wool www.toltyarnandwool.com

Wool Wash
Ecover Delicate Laundry Wash (available.from health food shops and supermarkets) www.uk.ecover.com
Soak Wash www.soakwash.com
Eucalan www.eucalan.com
Twig & Horn Wool Soap www.twigandhorn.com

Software
Knit Bird www.knitbird.com
Stitch Mastery www.stitchmastery.com

General
Clover Pompom Makers (widely available from many craft and knitting shops)
Yarn Substitution database www.yarnsub.com
The Campaign For Wool www.campaignforwool.org